Psalms
Of Comfort

Comforting Passages
From The Book Of Psalms

Barbara Jurgensen

CSS Publishing Company, Inc., Lima, Ohio

PSALMS OF COMFORT

Copyright © 2004 by
CSS Publishing Company, Inc.
Lima, Ohio

For more information about CSS Publishing Company resources, visit our website at www.csspub.com or e-mail us at custserv@csspub.com or call (800) 241-4056.

ISBN 0-7880-2335-7

PRINTED IN U.S.A.

Welcome to *Psalms Of Comfort.* In all the world there's no comfort greater than the comfort our Lord gives us in the book of Psalms.

Whether we're facing serious illness, the wrong-doing of others (or ourselves), or some terrible loss, Jesus reaches out his loving arms and says, "Come to me, all you who are weary and burdened, and I will give you rest."

He offers us forgiveness. And new life. And his peace, which passes all human understanding.

We can say, "Lord Jesus, come into my life. Forgive all my sin, and make me your beloved child. Lead me, guide me, give me a new purpose for living."

May you know our Lord's comfort as you invite him to strengthen you with the words of his mighty Psalms.

I'm grieving, Lord, because I've lost my closest friend. Day after day we talked together and did things together and shared our lives. How will I ever go on without her?

To you I call, O Lord my Rock ...

The Lord is my strength and my shield;

my heart trusts in him, and I am helped.

Psalm 28:1a, 7a

My friend was such an important part of my life. I need someone who understands me, and cares about me, and will walk my life journey with me — and I'll do the same for that friend. Aha ... you understand me even better, and care about me even more, and will always stick by me. You're an even greater Friend. Thank you, Jesus.

This is a frightening world, Lord. Sometimes when I lie down at night I'm so restless that it's hard to get to sleep.

I will lie down and sleep in peace,

for you alone, O Lord,

make me dwell in safety.

Psalm 4:8

I keep forgetting that you've invited us to cast all our cares upon you and you'll give us peace and rest, Jesus. And I know I don't have to be afraid of anything that might happen tomorrow because we'll be going there together. Thank you.

You've been working with us, Lord, refining us like precious metal, and this hasn't been easy for us. Sometimes, like blazing-hot iron plunged into icy water (in the process of being turned into fine surgical steel), we cry out.

Praise our God, O peoples ...

he has preserved our lives

    and kept our feet from slipping.

For you, O God, tested us;

    you refined us like silver.

                Psalm 66:8a, 9-10

Jesus, I know that you're totally caring, and that everything you do is to help us grow and, like fine surgical steel, be useful. Help us trust your loving purposes.

*L*ord, *I know that someday my time on this earth will end. That's a little frightening.*

The Lord is my shepherd, I shall not be in want.

He makes me lie down in green pastures,

he leads me beside quiet waters,

he restores my soul ...

Even though I walk through the valley

of the shadow of death,

I will fear no evil, for you are with me ...

Surely goodness and love will follow me

all the days of my life,

and I will dwell in the house of the Lord forever.

Psalm 23:1-3a, 4a, 6

Loving Lord Jesus, be my shepherd, always.

Lord, this world seems to be purposely steering itself farther away from you. The movies and television get raunchier, your name is trampled on, so few seem to want to follow you. How can I live in the midst of such darkness?

How lovely is your dwelling place,

    O Lord Almighty!

My soul yearns, even faints,

    for the courts of the Lord;

my heart and my flesh cry out

    for the living God.

Psalm 84:1-2

I love to come into your house, Jesus, and be among people who care about you and want to follow you. Show us how to live as your sons and daughters in the midst of this wayward world.

I'll be going in for surgery soon, Lord, and I guess you know how I'm feeling. What if things don't go the way I'm hoping? Help me, Lord! Help me!

You are the God who performs miracles;

you display your power among the peoples.

Psalm 77:14

Jesus, I need you to go through this with me, so let me reach out my hand whenever I need to and hold onto yours. Guide the doctors and nurses and all who'll be giving me care. And whatever the outcome, I know that you'll stay right here beside me. Help me put my trust in you.

*L*ord, someone I care about has gotten into
trouble, and it's hard to know how to help.

Hear my prayer, O Lord;

    let my cry for help come to you.

Turn your ear to me ...

        Psalm 102:1, 2b

*Jesus, show me how to best express my love and con-
cern, how to give them the support they need. But I
know that, most of all, they need you. We're all the
prodigal child, and you're our loving Father. Help
us, Lord.*

I'm feeling down, Lord, and nothing seems to help. I fret, and fuss, and stew. And then I stew some more.

Why are you downcast, O my soul?

Why so disturbed within me?

Put your hope in God ...

Psalm 42:5a

Jesus, why do I keep forgetting that I'm your beloved child? You know all about me, and yet you still love me, tenderly, fervently. And you've promised that you'll give me your joy — a deep, abiding joy that comes only from you. Lord, I need your joy. I need you.

*L*ord, how could there have been such a terrible accident? How could such a thing happen? And how can I go on?

God is our refuge and strength,

an ever-present help in trouble.

Therefore we will not fear,

though the earth give way

and the mountains fall into

the heart of the sea ...

Psalm 46:1-2

Jesus, I never thought such a terrible thing could happen to me. I don't know which way to turn, except to you. You've promised us that you'll never leave us or forsake us; I need you to stay close beside me now. Help me, Lord! Help me! I ask in your name.

13

*I'm so tired of being sick, Lord. Being patient —
and being a patient — is hard. Couldn't you heal
me right now?*

Be still before the Lord

and wait patiently for him ...

Psalm 37:7a

*I guess I have learned a few things while I've been
down. I've come to appreciate more the good things
in my life, like my family and friends. And I can see
now that possessions aren't as important as I used
to think. I've come closer to you, Jesus, which has
been the best part. So if you have more things to teach
me, could you help me be patient?*

Troubles keep coming at me, Lord, threatening to overwhelm me. If I do manage to get rid of one, two others attack. Help me!

Though I walk

in the midst of trouble,

you preserve my life ...

Psalm 138:7a

Loving Lord Jesus, I know that you had some purpose in mind when you created me — how amazing! And that you delight in each of us — even more amazing. Lead me, day by day, so that, in the midst of whatever troubles life may bring, I may fulfill your purpose — and experience your delight.

*L*ord, it's like the world's suddenly been pulled out from under me! How can I keep going? How can I possibly keep going? Help me!

I lift up my eyes to the hills —

    where does my help come from?

My help comes from the Lord,

    the Maker of heaven and earth ...

The Lord watches over you ...

the Lord will watch over your coming and going

    both now and forevermore.

Psalm 121:1-2, 5a, 8

Jesus, you've promised to be with us always. And you keep track of each tiny sparrow, so I know you're watching over me. Help me to trust you completely.

I've had such a deep longing for something, Lord, and I've tried so many different things, but nothing has ever satisfied this longing.

O God, you are my God,

    earnestly I seek you;

my soul thirsts for you,

    my body longs for you,

in a dry and weary land

    where there is no water.

Psalm 63:1

It's been a long search, and I keep coming up empty. Now I realize that what I've been longing for is you. Only you can give me the love, the joy, and the peace that I need — and the sense that my life has meaning. Come into my life, Jesus; forgive my sin, and be my Lord and Savior.

I'm feeling down, Lord. Some of the people I've counted on haven't done what they should. But I have to admit that I haven't always done what I should, either. All of us are muddling along.

Find rest, O my soul, in God alone;

my hope comes from him.

Psalm 62:5

It's been said that we're restless until we find our rest in you, Jesus. I think I've been looking for a solid footing in life in the wrong places. I know that nothing else, and no one else, is as trustworthy, or can give us the peace that you give us. I need you.

Lord, you know that today my doctor told me that I have a serious, life-threatening illness. I'm frightened! My whole world has fallen apart!

The Lord is my light and my salvation —

whom shall I fear?

The Lord is the stronghold of my life —

of whom shall I be afraid?

For in the day of trouble

he will keep me safe in his dwelling ...

Psalm 27:1, 5a

Jesus, promise me that you'll go through this with me. Wait, I already have your promise that that's exactly what you'll do. And that in all things you'll work for good for those who love you and are called according to your purpose. Thank you.

*L*ord, our family's going through a terrible time. A desperately terrible time. Help us!

Help us, O God our Savior,

    for the glory of your name;

deliver us and forgive our sins

    for your name's sake ...

may your mercy come quickly to meet us,

    for we are in desperate need.

Psalm 79:9, 8b

I don't see how things could get much worse. And nothing we've tried seems to help. I think what we really need is you, Jesus.

J esus, I've been so sick. Some days I'm afraid I won't live, and some days I'm afraid I will. What good is my life? And does anyone else really care? Help me, Lord!

For he will deliver the needy who cry out,

the afflicted who have no one to help.

Psalm 72:12

Loving Lord, when I stop to think about it, I know that I'm not alone; you're right here with me, and you've given me your Holy Spirit so I have the power to do your work with you, and your angels to watch over me. There are those who care about me — and even some who need me. You may yet have work for me to do, so give me the strength to hold on and follow you. Thank you.

I'm bent over, dragged down, weary, Lord. Sometimes it feels like I'm carrying the weight of the world on my shoulders. Help!

Cast your cares on the Lord

and he will sustain you ...

Psalm 55:22a

Why am I carrying this heavy burden when you've invited me to give it to you? Jesus, take it, please. I know you lifted my heaviest load when you took all our sinfulness to the cross, so that whoever believes in you shall have eternal life. Thank you.

Lord, I'm tired of hearing the newspapers and television telling about yet another high-ranking person who's gone astray. Who can we count on any more?

Send forth your light and your truth,

let them guide me;

let them bring me to your holy mountain,

to the place where you dwell.

Psalm 43:3

I'm glad that we'll always be able to depend on you, Jesus. You are truth. And light. And life itself. The worse things get here on this earth, the more I appreciate you.

L ord, I'm in deep trouble. The merciless flood waters of this life are trying to engulf me, and I'm about to sink. Help me!

Save me, O God,

for the waters have come up to my neck.

I sink in the miry depths,

where there is no foothold.

Answer me, O Lord, out of the goodness

of your love ...

Psalm 69:1-2a, 16a

Jesus, don't let the problems of this world drag me down to the depths. Out of the great goodness of your love, help me. And remind me that you'll be with me here, and I'll be with you in your house forever.

*L*ord, how could someone I cared about so much be gone? I feel like I've been dropped into a deep pit, and terrible darkness is pressing in on me from all sides. Help me!

Out of the depths I cry to you, O Lord;

O Lord, hear my voice.

I wait for the Lord, my soul waits,

and in his word I put my hope.

Psalm 130:1-2a, 5

Jesus, you've promised us that you'll be very near to the brokenhearted. That you'll console all who mourn. And that you'll give us your peace, a peace that no one else can give. I need you, Lord. Be very near to me.

*S*omeone *I trusted has turned against me, Lord, and I'm hurt — badly hurt. I want to lash out; I want to rage at them.*

Trouble and distress

 have come upon me,

but your commands

 are my delight.

 Psalm 119:143

Jesus, keep me from repaying anger with anger. Show me how to deal with this person with your kind of love. And thank you for being the friend who never lets me down.

In Bible times, people could run to cities of refuge to escape those who wanted to do them harm. Lord, you've promised to be such a place of protection for us, and I need such a place now.

In you, O Lord, I have taken refuge ...

Be my rock of refuge,

   to which I can always go ...

Psalm 71:1a, 3a

Jesus, where else can I go? Only you can give me the help I need. Help me, Lord, help me!

*L*ord, people are saying things about me that aren't true. Cruel things. Hateful things. Things I would never do. Help me!

I have set the Lord always before me.

Because he is at my right hand,

I will not be shaken.

Psalm 16:8

I just remembered what you said in the Beatitudes: "Blessed are you when people insult you, persecute you and falsely say all kinds of evil against you because of me. Rejoice and be glad, because great is your reward in heaven, for in the same way they persecuted the prophets who were before you." Help me be at peace in you, Jesus.

Pain has been beating on me, Lord. Constant, wall-to-wall pain. It's wearing me down, sapping my strength. Help me!

I will be glad and rejoice in your love,

for you saw my affliction

and knew the anguish of my soul.

Psalm 31:7

When I cried out to you, you took my burden on your own shoulders, and I knew that I wouldn't have to go on carrying it by myself. The greatest thing in all creation is your tender love for us, Jesus. Nothing else even comes close. Thank you.

Lord, I know that things will not go on as they are forever. I've come to the point in my life where I need to make some important arrangements. Help me.

Into your hands

I commit my spirit;

redeem me, O Lord ...

Psalm 31:5

Jesus, thank you for who and what you are. It's so good to know that I can trust everything that I am and have into your loving care. Thank you.

*L*ife's been difficult, Lord. You know how things were in the family where I grew up. And my physical problems. And the other things I've struggled with. How could all this happen to me when I've been trying to follow you?

How great is your goodness,

which you have stored up

for those who fear you ...

Psalm 31:19a

Then I remember Sarah and Abraham, Mary and Joseph, and all your faithful people through the ages. Their lives were not easy. In fact, their lives were probably more difficult because they wanted to live as your people — the cost of discipleship. Walk beside me, Jesus, and keep me on the path, wherever it may lead.

31

*I 've had to face many fierce storms in my life, Lord,
and I'm afraid there'll be more to come. How will
I ever be able to make it through them?*

Your path led through the sea,

   your way through the mighty waters,

   though your footprints were not seen.

You led your people like a flock ...

Psalm 77:19-20a

*Lead me, Jesus, through the troubled waters of this
life just as you led your people through the dark
waters of the Egyptian sea. Keep me in your loving
care. Help me share your love and concern with the
people around me, and bring me home at last. I ask
in your name. Amen.*

Das Mädchen mit den 200 Schmusetieren

Du même auteur

Certaines œuvres sont connues sous différents titres.

Romans

La Faute à Souchon : (Le roman du show-biz et de la sagesse)
Quand les familles sans toit sont entrées dans les maisons fermées
Liberté j'ignorais tant de Toi (Libertés d'avant l'an 2000)
Viré, viré, viré, même viré du Rmi !
Ils ne sont pas intervenus (Peut-être un roman autobiographique)

Théâtre

Neuf femmes et la star
Les secrets de maître Pierre, notaire de campagne
Ça magouille aux assurances
Chanteur, écrivain : même cirque
Deux sœurs et un contrôle fiscal
Amour, sud et chansons
Pourquoi est-il venu :
Aventures d'écrivains régionaux
Avant les élections présidentielles
Scènes de campagne, scènes du Quercy
Blaise Pascal serait webmaster
Trois femmes et un Amour
J'avais 25 ans
« Révélations » sur « les apparitions d'Astaffort » Jacques Brel Francis Cabrel

Théâtre pour troupes d'enfants

La fille aux 200 doudous
Les filles en profitent
Révélations sur la disparition du père Noël
Le lion l'autruche et le renard,
Mertilou prépare l'été
Nous n'irons plus au restaurant

4

Stéphane Ternoise

Übersetzung :
Jeanne Meurtin

Das Mädchen mit den 200 Schmusetieren

Mo, 17. Oktober 2011

Theatersammlung

Französische Veröffentlichung :
La fille aux 200 doudous

Jean-Luc PETIT Editeur / Collection THEATRE

Stéphane Ternoise
versant
théâtre :

http://www.dramaturge.fr

Das Mädchen mit den 200 Schmusetieren

Verteilung :

Von sechs bis etwa 20 Kindern.

Szene :

In ihrem Bett, ein 6-7 jähriges kleines Mädchen, kaum sichtbar. Zu viele Schmusetiere! Schmusetiere gibt es auch im ganzen Zimmer. Einige Kinder (fünf minimum, gleichaltrig) treten auf Zehenspitzen ein. Sie beobachten, bewundern, lächeln sich an, begeistern sich, zeigen sich die Schmusetiere.

Das Mädchen mit den 200 Schmusetieren

Erster Akt

Erstes Kind : - In ihrem Zimmer kann man kaum treten.

Zweites Kind : - Sogar ihr Kopfkissen wird überschwemmt.

Drittes Kind : - Ihre Regale sind ja schlimmer als die meiner Großmutter mit ihren Marmeladengläsern.

Viertes Kind : - Schlimmer als die meines Großvaters mit seinem Werkzeugkasten.

Anderes Kind : - Schlimmer als Mutters Kleiderschrank.

Das kleine Mädchen sitzt auf dem Bett, und bemerkt, dass die anderen da sind.

Drittes Kind : - Sie ist das Mädchen mit den 200 Schmusetieren, die ist komisch, die ist komisch.

Anderes Kind, raunend : - Sie ist das Mädchen mit den 200 Schmusetieren, die sind komisch, die sind komisch.

Viertes Kind : - Sie ist das Mädchen mit den

200 Schmusetieren, jede Hosenmatz ist auf sie neidisch.

Das kleine Mädchen vom Bett : - Seid ihr nicht darauf neidisch, liebe Freunde ? Glaubt ihr vielleicht, dass man sich keine Sorgen macht, wenn man vom morgens bis abends 200 Schmusetiere beaufsichtigen muss ? Sogar vom Abend bis zum Morgen.

Viertes Kind : - Solche Sorgen hätte ich gern !

Das kleine Mädchen vom Bett : - Das ist doch nicht so lustig, wenn sich Mäuschen hinter Vati Elefant versteckt, obwohl er bei seiner zärtlichen Mutti schlafen sollte. Und denkt ihr etwa, dass jeder am Abend gleichzeitig müde ist ? Das ist doch schlimmer als einen Schlafraum für Schulmädchen.

Viertes Kind : - Schlafraum für Schulmädchen gibt es nicht !

Zweites Kind : - Oma hat mir erzählt : Vor langer Zeit, viel früher als 2000, gingen die Kinder nicht nach Hause zurück, sondern blieben in der Schule in einem Schlafraum.

Viertes Kind : - In einem Schlafraum ! Wie gemein waren ihre Eltern !

Zweites Kind : - Ne Dummkopf ! Es könnte nicht anders sein, es gab kein Bus !

Viertes Kind : - Hör auf mit dem Quark.

Das kleine Mädchen vom Bett : - Es mag erstaunlich sein, aber es ist wahr. Und die Kinder hatten damals nicht immer Schmusetiere wie wir. Viele sind mit kleinen Schmusetüchern zufrieden.

Viertes Kind : - Ich hätte mich geweigert zu schlafen ! Ich hätte demonstriert ! Ich hätte geschrien !

Anderes Kind : - Ich hätte gebissen !

Viertes Kind : - Ich wäre zu Oma gezogen !

Erstes Kind, *geht zu einem Regal und nimmt einen Plüschhund* : - Wie heißt er ?

Das kleine Mädchen vom Bett : - Jeder hat seinen Spitznamen, von Lampenschirm bis zu Zombou. Was ihn betrifft, er heißt Scott-Key.

Erstes Kind : - Scott-Key ?

Das kleine Mädchen vom Bett : - Ich vermute, dass du weder deinen Namen, noch den Vornamen, noch den Spitznamen gewählt hast. So ist es ! Er war ein ausgesetzter Hund. *Träumerisch, leise* : - Ich war vier Jahre alt : es regnete und er weinte vor dem Schaufenster eines Geschäfts.

Viertes Kind, *zu seinem Nachbar* : - Ein Schmusetier weint doch nicht !

Das kleine Mädchen vom Bett, *die zuhört und sich zu ihm wendet* : - Du hast schon vergessen, dass ein Schmusetier weinen darf !

Sie erzählt seine Geschichte weiter. Er weinte vor dem Schaufenster eines Geschäftes, ein Schildchen hing an seinen rechten Ohr, ein mieses gelbes Schildchen mit fünf schwarzen Grossbuchstaben : S-a-l-e-s.

Erstes Kind : - Wusstest du denn nicht, was Sales bedeutet ?

Das kleine Mädchen vom Bett : - Ich war vier Jahre alt, das darfst Du nicht vergessen ! Natürlich habe ich meinen Vati gezwungen,

11

einzutreten. Stolz mit meinen vier Jahren habe ich die Verkäuferin gerade in die Augen geschaut und gefragt : „Heißt er echt Sales ?".

Erstes Kind : - Konntest du schon lesen ?

Das kleine Mädchen vom Bett : - Mein lieber Vati hat mit mir einen Deal gemacht : - Ich kaufe dir einen Schmusetier und du hast Rechtschreibeunterricht jeden Abend, bevor ich dir eine Geschichte vorlese. So konnte ich im Alter von dreieinhalb fast alles lesen.

Erstes Kind : - Du dachtest doch, dass Sales sein Name war !

Das kleine Mädchen vom Bett : - Hast du nie Fehler gemacht, die du heute lachhaft findest ?

Erstes Kind : - Ich wollte nur prüfen, dass du kein Wunderkind bist ! Tja, hat die Verkäuferin deinen Vati fragend angelächelt oder hat sie dir geantwortet ?

Das kleine Mädchen vom Bett : - Mir wurde immer geantwortet, als ich vier war und vor allem wenn ich den Personen gerade in die Augen schaute. Weißt du, so. *Sie starrt ihn an.*

Drittes Kind : - Sie hat „eine Marsbewohnerin" geschrien !

Das kleine Mädchen vom Bett : - Äh...

Drittes Kind : - Was äh ?...

Das kleine Mädchen vom Bett : - Tja. Ohne wegzugucken hat die Verkäuferin geantwortet : „ äh..." Dann habe ich ihr erklärt : Sehen Sie, ich habe schon ein Schmusetier, der Sales heißt. Es ist ein geliebter roter Frosch. Und... Obwohl ich ihn adoptieren möchte, hätte ich Angst davor, dass wir im Zimmer uns verwechseln.

Drittes Kind : - Sie war überhaupt überrascht, dass du schon lesen kannst !

Viertes Kind : - Hat sie über dich lustig gemacht ?

Das kleine Mädchen vom Bett : - Gar nicht, böses Kind ! Sie hat mir höflich geantwortet:" Sein echter Name ist Scott-Key"... Dann hat sie leiser gesagt:" Meine Kollegin hat einen Fehler gemacht."

Zweites Kind : - So hat dein Vati ihn dir gekauft !

Das kleine Mädchen vom Bett : - Wie hast du das erraten ? Doch zuvor habe ich gefragt : „Und wie buchstabieren sie es ? „. Dann habe ich dieses neue Wort in meinem Heft aufgeschrieben. *Sie zieht ihr Heft vom Nachtisch und blättert zärtlich darin.*

Zweites Kind : - Was bedeutet Scott-Key ?

Das kleine Mädchen vom Bett : - Geheimnis !

Viertes Kind : - Du sagt das, weil du davon nichts weißt !

Das kleine Mädchen vom Bett : - Du bist doch wie zweideutig als einen fliegenden Fisch.

Viertes Kind : - Na los, gib uns die Lösung !

Das kleine Mädchen vom Bett : - Sogar mit den Schmusetieren darf das Geheimnis mit der Wahl der Spitznamen bestehen !

13

Chor von den Kindern :

Sie ist das Mädchen mit den 200 Schmusetieren, die ist komisch, die ist komisch. Sie ist das Mädchen mit den 200 Schmusetieren, jeder Hosenmatz ist neidisch. Sie ist das Mädchen mit den 200 Schmusetieren, sie ist geheimnistuerisch.

Drittes Kind : - Wie findest du dich zurecht ?

Das kleine Mädchen vom Bett : - Früher war Montag den Tag der weißen Schmusetiere, Dienstag maulen, Mittwoch braunen, Donnerstag gelben, Freitag grünen, Samstag sandfarbigen und Sonntag war für die anderen Farben.

Zweites Kind : - Montag war der König !

Das kleine Mädchen vom Bett : - Jetzt heißen die Wochentage Tage für Kaninchen, Katzen, Enten, Bärchen, Wauwau und der Wunderlichkeiten.

Viertes Kind : - Und der siebte Tag ?

Das kleine Mädchen vom Bett : - Du kannst ja rechnen ! Ach, der siebte Tag...

Die Kinder : - Oh, erzähl mal !

Das kleine Mädchen vom Bett : - Der siebte Tag ist ein bisschen speziell im neuen Schmusetierskalender... Er ist der Tag der Wahlen.

Die Kinder : - Wahlen !?

Das kleine Mädchen vom Bett : - Mit

14

Abstimmung durch Beinaufheben entschieden sich die Schmusetiere, wer gefeiert wird.

Viertes Kind : - Was wird gewonnen?

Das kleine Mädchen vom Bett : - Das Schönste der Geschenke!

Ein Kind : - Ein Anzug von Zorro?

Das kleine Mädchen vom Bette zuckt mit den Achseln.
Antworte kommen aus allen Richtungen.
Sie sieht sehr enttäuscht aus.

Ein Kind : - Ein Schal? Ein Bandana-Tuch?

Ein Kind : - Ein Erdbeeryogurt?

Ein Kind : - Kügelchen?

Ein Kind : - Ein Gameboy?

Ein Kind : - Ein Puzzle... von bayerischen Schweinen?

Ein Kind : - Eine... schweizer Schokoladentafel?

Während der Aufführungen können andere Antworte, nach den Nachrichten oder Geschmäcken, hinzugefügt werden.

Ein Kind : - Na los, sag uns...

Das kleine Mädchen vom Bett : - Das schönste der Geschenke, wovon ein Schmusetier träumen kann. Der Gewinner schläft in meinen Armen.

Viertes Kind, *ganz spontan* : - darf ich an den Wahlen teilnehmen?

15

Das Kleine Mädchen vom Bett lächelt ihn an.
Jeder schaut ihn an. Er sieht gezwungen aus.

Drittes Kind : - Schläfst du noch mit einem Schmusetier in den Armen ?

Das kleine Mädchen vom Bett : - Du nicht ?

Drittes Kind : - Äh... *Jeder schaut sie an.*

Drittes Kind : -Normaleweise ist es noch ein Geheimnis.

Drittes Kind : - Schläfst du noch mit einem Schmusetier in den Armen ?

Das kleine Mädchen vom Bett : - Wenn jemand sich über dich lustig macht, weil du mit einem Schmusetier in den Armen schläfst, frag dir, wenn er am Abend mit jeden Sekunden zufrieden ist.

Anderes Kind : - Aber eines Tages werden deine Schmusetiere auf den Dachboden gehen, oder ?

Das kleine Mädchen vom Bett : - Älter werden bedeutet nicht nur weg von Schmusetieren sein. Sie verleugnen überhaupt nicht !

Chor von den Kindern :

Sie ist das Mädchen mit den 200 Schmusetieren, die ist komisch, die ist komisch.
Sie ist das Mädchen mit den 200 Schmusetieren, jeder Hosenmatz ist neidisch.

16

Sie ist das Mädchen mit den 200 Schmusetieren, ein Schmusetierestammtisch.

Das kleine Mädchen vom Bett : - Ach. Schmusetiere, die Pause ist zu Ende gekommen. Hört auf, für Kinder zu halten ! *Sie wendet sich einen Fuchs zu.* Ich möchte gern ein bisschen schlafen. Du übertriebst !

Das vierte Kind tritt durch die Tür, schüchternd, hüstelt ein bisschen, um ihre Aufmerksamkeit auf sich zu lenken.

Viertes Kind : - Fräulein, Fräulein... *Das kleine Mädchen wendet sich ihn zu und lächelt ihn an.* Ich war ehrlich, als ich von den Wahlen gesprochen habe. **Das kleine Mädchen vom Bett** : - Ich weiß, ich weiß... Aber wenn du den Kaninchen und Bärchenwahlen nicht hast, hast du keine Chance zu gewinnen... *Das vierte Kind ist traurig.* In zehn Jahren vielleicht werde ich die einzige Wählerin sein.

Ende

17

Stéphane Ternoise...

Ternoise Stéphane ist ein französischer Schriftsteller.

Er wurde 1968 geboren. Er veröffentlicht seit 1991.

Katalog und Website :
http://www.ecrivain.pro

Spielen Sie dieses Spiel...

Um diesen Teil, um Erlaubnis zu spielen:
http://www.franzoesischestheater.com

Texte en français

La fille aux 200 doudous

Pièce pour enfants en un acte

Distribution :

Six à une vingtaine d'enfants.

Scène : dans son lit, une fillette, 6-7 ans, à peine visible. Trop de doudous ! Des doudous aussi dans toute la chambre. Entrent des enfants (minimum cinq, même âge), sur la pointe des pieds. Ils observent, admirent, se sourient, s'extasient, se montrent des doudous.

La fille aux 200 doudous

Acte 1

1er enfant : - Dans sa chambre, on avance au p'tit bonheur la chance.

2eme enfant : - Même son oreiller est envahi.

3eme enfant : - Ses étagères, c'est pire que ma grand-mère avec ses pots de confiture.

4eme enfant : - C'est pire que mon grand-père avec ses boîtes à outils.

Autre enfant : - Pire que la garde-robe de maman

La fillette du lit sourit, comme si elle s'apercevait seulement à l'instant de leur présence.

3eme enfant : - C'est la fille aux 200 doudous, y'en a partout, y'en a partout.

Autre enfant reprend en murmurant : - C'est la fille aux 200 doudous, y'en a partout, y'en a partout.

4eme enfant : - C'est la fille aux 200 doudous, tous les p'tits loups en sont jaloux.

La fillette du lit : - Ne soyez pas jaloux, mes amis. Vous croyez peut-être qu'on n'a pas ses petits soucis, quand on doit surveiller du matin au soir 200 doudous ? Et même du soir au matin.

4eme enfant : - Des soucis comme ça, j'aimerais bien en avoir.

23

La fillette du lit : - Pourtant, ce n'est pas spécialement drôle, quand souriceau se cache derrière papa éléphant alors qu'il devrait dormir près de sa tendre maman. Et la nuit, vous croyez peut-être que tous ont sommeil en même temps ? C'est pire qu'un dortoir d'écolières.

4eme enfant : - Un dortoir d'écolières, ça n'existe pas !

2eme enfant : - Mamie m'a raconté : il y a très très longtemps, c'était bien avant l'an 2000, les enfants ne rentraient pas chez eux le soir mais restaient dormir à l'école, dans un dortoir.

4eme enfant : - Un dortoir ! Comme leurs parents étaient méchants !

2eme enfant : - Mais non grand bêta, ce n'était pas possible autrement, il n'y avait pas de bus.

4eme enfant : - Arrête de raconter des blagues.

La fillette du lit : - C'est peut-être surprenant mais c'est pourtant vrai. Et les enfants n'ont pas toujours eu des doudous comme nous, beaucoup se contentaient d'un simple chiffon.

4eme enfant : - J'aurais refusé de dormir ! J'aurais manifesté ! J'aurais crié !

Autre enfant : - J'aurais pincé !

4eme enfant : - J'aurais déménagé chez grand-mère !

1er enfant, *va vers une étagère et prend un chien en peluche* : - Il s'appelle comment ?

La fillette du lit : - Chacun a son surnom, d'abat-jour à zombou. Quant à lui, c'est Scott-Key.

1er enfant : - Scott-Key ?

La fillette du lit : - Je suppose que tu n'as pas choisi ton nom, pas même ton prénom ni ton surnom. Hé bien lui, c'était un chien abandonné. *(rêveuse, doucement :)* J'avais quatre ans : il pleuvait, et lui pleurait à la vitrine d'un magasin,

4eme enfant *(à son voisin)* : - Ça ne pleure pas un doudou !

La fillette du lit, *qui a entendu, se tourne vers lui* : - Tu as déjà oublié qu'un doudou, parfois, ça pleure ! *(reprenant l'histoire)* il pleurait à la vitrine d'un magasin, avec une étiquette à l'oreille droite, une vilaine étiquette jaune avec 5 lettres majuscules noires : s-o-l-d-e.

1er enfant : - Et toi, tu ne savais pas que ça voulait dire SOLDE !

La fillette du lit : - J'avais quatre ans, ne l'oubliez pas quand même ! Forcément, j'ai forcé mon papa à entrer, et avec toute la fierté de mes quatre ans, j'ai demandé à la vendeuse, en la regardant bien droit dans les yeux « il s'appelle vraiment solde ? »

1er enfant : - Tu savais déjà lire ?

La fillette du lit : - Ça c'est une combine de mon papa adoré ! Je t'achète un doudou mais

25

cours d'orthographe chaque soir, avant la lecture d'une histoire. C'est ainsi qu'à trois ans et demi je savais presque tout lire.

1er enfant : - Mais tu croyais que SOLDE, c'était son nom !

La fillette du lit : - N'as-tu jamais fait d'erreurs qu'aujourd'hui tu trouves plus grotesques ?

1er enfant : - C'était juste pour vérifier que tu n'étais pas une petite génie ! Bon, alors, la vendeuse, elle a souri en interrogeant ton papa du regard ou elle t'a répondu ?

La fillette du lit : - On me répondait toujours, quand j'avais quatre ans et que je regardais droit dans les yeux, tu vois, comme ça (*elle le fixe*).

3eme enfant : - Elle a hurlé « une martienne » !

La fillette du lit : - Euh...

3eme enfant : - Quoi euh ?...

La fillette du lit : - Bin la vendeuse, sans détourner les yeux, a répondu : « euh... » Alors je lui ai expliqué, comme on parle à une vendeuse qui n'a rien compris : « vous voyez, j'ai déjà un doudou prénommé SOLDE, une adorable grenouille rouge cerise Burlat, alors, bien que je souhaite l'adopter, j'aurais trop peur que ça crée de la confusion dans ma chambre. »

3eme enfant : - Elle était surtout surprise que tu saches déjà lire !

4eme enfant : - Elle s'est moquée de toi ?

La fillette du lit : - Pas du tout, petit impertinent ! Elle m'a répondu poliment, « son véritable nom c'est Scott-Key »… et un ton en dessous, « c'est une erreur de ma collègue. »

2eme enfant : - Alors ton papa te l'a acheté !

La fillette du lit : - Comment as-tu deviné ? Mais avant j'ai demandé, « et vous écrivez ça comment », alors j'ai noté ce mot nouveau dans mon carnet (*elle prend le carnet sur la table de nuit, le feuillette tendrement*).

2eme enfant : - Ça veut dire quoi, Scott-Key ?

La fillette du lit : - Secret !

4eme enfant : - Tu réponds ça car tu n'en sais rien !

La fillette du lit : - Mais tu es aussi polisson que les bébés hérissons.

4eme enfant : - Allez, donne-nous la solution.

La fillette du lit : - Même au sujet des doudous, il doit rester un peu de mystère dans le choix des surnoms.

Chœur des enfants :

C'est la fille aux 200 doudous, y'en a partout, y'en a partout.
C'est la fille aux 200 doudous, tous les p'tits loups en sont jaloux.
C'est la fille aux 200 doudous, ses secrets sont pas pour nous.

3eme enfant : - Comment tu te repères ?

27

La fillette du lit : - Avant, c'était lundi doudous blancs, mardi mauves, mercredi marron, jeudi jaunes, vendredi verts, samedi sable et dimanche autres couleurs.
2eme enfant : - Le lundi était roi !
La fillette du lit : - Maintenant, les jours de la semaine s'appellent fête des lapins, des chats, des canards. Fête des oursons, des toutous et des bizarres.
4eme enfant : - Et le septième jour ?
La fillette du lit : - Monsieur sait compter ! Ah ! Le septième jour...
Les enfants : - Oh raconte !...
La fillette du lit : - Le septième jour est... un peu spécial dans le nouveau calendrier des doudous... c'est le jour des élections.
Les enfants : - Des élections !?
La fillette du lit : - Par un vote, naturellement à pattes levées, les doudous décident qui sera célébré.
4eme enfant : - Y'a quoi à gagner ?
La fillette du lit : - Le plus beau des cadeaux !
Un enfant : - Une tenue de Zorro ?

La fillette du lit hausse les épaules.
Les réponses fusent à son grand désappointement :
Un enfant : - Une écharpe ? Un bandana ?

Un enfant : - Un yaourt aux fraises ?
Un enfant : - Des billes ?

28

Un enfant : - Une game boy ?

Un enfant : - Un puzzle... de cochons des Pyrénées ?

Un enfant : - Une plaque de chocolat... suisse ?

(lors des représentations, d'autres réponses, suivant les goûts et l'actualité, peuvent être ajoutées, préférées)

Un enfant : - Allez, dis-nous...

La fillette du lit : - Le plus beau des cadeaux dont peut rêver un doudou... le gagnant dort dans mes bras.

4eme enfant *spontanément* : - Je peux participer aux élections ?

La fillette du lit lui sourit ; tous le regardent ; il est gêné.

3eme enfant : - Tu dors encore avec un doudou dans les bras !

La fillette du lit : - Pas toi ?

3eme enfant : - Eh... *(tous la regardent)*

3eme enfant : - Mais normalement c'est un secret.

La fillette du lit : - Si quelqu'un rit de toi parce que tu dors avec un doudou dans les bras, demande-toi s'il profite vraiment de chaque seconde de sa nuit.

Autre enfant : - Et un jour, tes doudous iront au grenier ?

La fillette du lit : - Grandir, ce n'est pas forcément s'éloigner de ses doudous, et surtout pas les renier !

Chœur des enfants :
C'est la fille aux 200 doudous, y'en a partout, y'en a partout.
C'est la fille aux 200 doudous, tous les p'tits loups en sont jaloux.
C'est la fille aux 200 doudous, et nous avons rendez-vous avec nos doudous.

Ils sortent de scène (en courant sur la pointe des pieds).

La fillette du lit : - Bon, maintenant, les doudous, la récréation est terminée. On arrête de se prendre pour des enfants (*se tournant vers un renard*) : j'aimerais bien dormir, moi, quand même, un peu. Il exagère ce monsieur Renardo des Forêts d'étagères.

Le 4eme enfant passe la tête à la porte, gêné, toussote un peu, sans parvenir à attirer l'attention. Timidement.

4eme enfant : - Mademoiselle, mademoiselle... (*la fillette se tourne vers lui et lui sourit*)
4eme enfant : - C'était pour de vrai, quand j'ai parlé des élections.

La fillette du lit : - Je sais, je sais... mais si tu n'as pas les voix des lapins et des ours, tu n'as aucune chance de gagner... (*le quatrième enfant est triste*) peut-être que dans dix ans, je serai la seule électrice.

Rideau - Fin

Die gesetzlichen...

Dépôt légal à la publication au format ebook du 17 octobre 2011

Imprimé par CreateSpace, An Amazon.com Company pour le compte de l'auteur-éditeur indépendant.
livrepapier.com

ISBN 978-2-36541-590-3
EAN 9782365415903
Das Mädchen mit den 200 Schmusetieren von Stéphane Ternoise, Übersetzung : Jeanne Meurtin
© Jean-Luc PETIT Editions - BP 17 - 46800 Montcuq - France – Frankreich

32

www.ingramcontent.com/pod-product-compliance
Lightning Source LLC
Chambersburg PA
CBHW071804020426

42331CB00008B/2399